A PICTURE & ACTIVITY BOOK

The Wild Wonders of
ALABAMA

BY C. E. MOORE

DEDICATED TO:
JAIME, COURTNEY, AND LORA

ABOUT THIS BOOK

This book celebrates the wild things. If we take the time to look closely, we'll see that our natural world is bursting with vibrancy. The millions of interactions of minerals, seeds, and spores cause things to bloom, decay, and erode. And, if we listen closely, we might hear the creatures of these wild places — the commotion of chirps, croaks, buzzes, and hisses.

This book seeks to inspire action for a more sustainable future. When we begin to understand that we're only one part of this wonderful and weird, giant ecosystem, we will realize the costs of our actions. If we're not good caretakers of nature, we can cause major disruptions to, or worse, elimination of, other species.

This book explores biodiversity, the amazing variety of life! You'll go on a sensory journey through three remarkable wild places selected for the unique nature within them. Additional natural treasures in Alabama can be found in the sections "Water," "Plant," "Animal," and "Call to Wild," which I hope will inspire you to learn even more about Alabama's amazing wildlife.

Come explore Alabama — its deep, rugged canyons and ancient, 500-million-year-old rock formations will captivate you! You will learn about a lost world full of botanical treasures, a bog abounding in predatory plants, and so much more!

I invite you to take a closer look at the beauty and intricacy of nature's wonders happening all around you.

C. E. Moore

Throughout this book:

Any yellow-highlighted words can be found in the glossary on page 40.

The conservation status of a species is an indicator of whether it exists and how likely it is to become extinct. This book uses status rankings from NatureServe (see table on right for definitions of rankings).

A common name along with the genus and species names identifies each plant and animal. See "Biological Classification," page 42, to learn more.

Common Name ⟶ **Black Bear** (S) ⟵ Status Ranking
Ursus americanus
↑ ↑
Genus   Species
Binomial Naming System

NATURESERVE CONSERVATION STATUS

(G1) Critically Imperiled, globally
(S1) Critically Imperiled, state level
At very high risk of extinction or elimination

(G2) Imperiled
(S2) Imperiled, state level
At high risk of extinction or elimination

(G3) Vulnerable
(S3) Vulnerable, state level
At moderate risk of extinction or elimination

(S) Secure

For a complete list of rankings, visit:
https://bit.ly/305r0UQ

TABLE OF CONTENTS

ALABAMA AT A GLANCE

 LOCATION

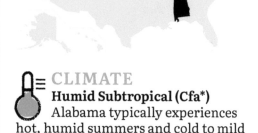

CLIMATE
Humid Subtropical (Cfa*)
Alabama typically experiences hot, humid summers and cold to mild winters with year-round rainfall.

*Köppen–Geiger climate classification system

SIX ECOREGIONS

View the map on page 5 to see where these ecoregions are located.

Basic Characteristics:

1 **Interior Low Plateau:** limestone plains and rugged hills

2 **Southwestern Appalachians:** rolling terrain rising to 1,800 feet above sea level

3 **Ridge and Valley:** steep, sandstone ridges and fertile limestone valleys

4 **Piedmont:** contains the oldest surface rocks in the state

5 **Southeastern Coastal Plain:** varying landscapes of swamps, wiregrass, and pine forests

6 **Southern Coastal Plain:** varying wetlands of estuaries, salt marshes, bayous, and river deltas

Explore Further, page 44.
"Weather vs. Climate"
"Ecoregions"

Flamed Tigersnail **S1**
Anguispira alternata

Did you know that 43 percent of all snail species that exist in the United States can be found in Alabama?

Alabama also has around 180 species of mussels — in fact, this state not only ranks the highest in species of snails and mussels but in crayfish and freshwater fish species, too!

Overall, Alabama ranks in the top five states for biodiversity. Why does it have such a diverse number of plant and animal species? While there are many factors, three major components are as follows:

Ample sunlight — Rainfall that evaporates from the Gulf of Mexico creates a warm, wet climate, which extends the growing season and thus creates more plant life.

Diverse geology — The formation of the Appalachian Mountains over time created a variety of bedrock and soil types that provide different types of habitats for plant and animal species to thrive.

Water — The state has extensive waterways — about 500,000 acres of standing water including rivers, lakes, bays, bayous, and other bodies of water. Different types of water allow for different types of species.

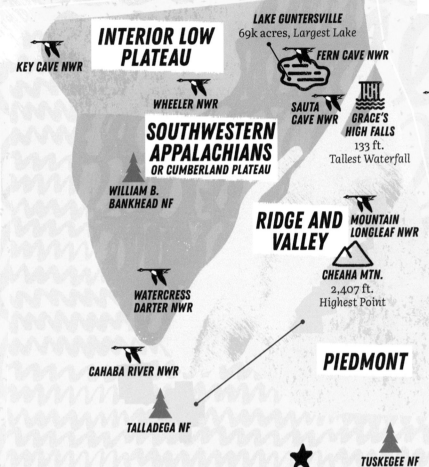

TN

INTERIOR LOW PLATEAU

KEY CAVE NWR

LAKE GUNTERSVILLE
69k acres, Largest Lake

FERN CAVE NWR

WHEELER NWR

SAUTA CAVE NWR

GRACE'S HIGH FALLS
133 ft.
Tallest Waterfall

SOUTHWESTERN APPALACHIANS
OR CUMBERLAND PLATEAU

WILLIAM B. BANKHEAD NF

RIDGE AND VALLEY

MOUNTAIN LONGLEAF NWR

CHEAHA MTN.
2,407 ft.
Highest Point

WATERCRESS DARTER NWR

MS

CAHABA RIVER NWR

PIEDMONT

TALLADEGA NF

MONTGOMERY

TUSKEGEE NF

EUFAULA NWR

SOUTHEASTERN COASTAL PLAIN

CHOCTAW NWR

GA

CONECUH NF

SOUTHERN COASTAL PLAIN

FL

GRAND BAY NWR

BON SECOUR NWR

GULF OF MEXICO

---

6 Ecoregions

4 National Forests (NF)
668,000 acres
fs.usda.gov

11 National Wildlife Refuges (NWR)
77,600 acres
fws.gov/refuges

(Not mapped)
21 State Parks
48,000 acres
alapark.com

4 State Forests
14,500 acres
nationalforests.org

36 Wildlife Management Areas
768,000 acres
outdooralabama.com

19 Alliance-Member Land Trusts
1,500,000 acres
landtrustalliance.org

Information subject to change. For current findings, please check with each organization.

Source: Level III ecoregions defined by the Environmental Protection Agency ● epa.gov

YOUR JOURNEY

Known for your keen observation skills, you've been asked by a wildlife expert to create an exciting project that highlights Alabama's wildlife for your friends!

To get a good, general sense of the state's biodiversity, your journey will consist of two segments: *PART ONE* explores wildlife in three specific places while *PART TWO* provides a snapshot of the flora and fauna across the state.

Along the way, you'll learn about various scientists and their work in the field (see the first one below). At journey's end, you'll have the opportunity to get creative and share your own voice about a topic of your choosing on pages 35–37.

Read below for your route along with a few starter questions to think about as you embark on your wild adventure!

 1 LITTLE RIVER CANYON NATIONAL PRESERVE

The journey begins in the Southwestern Appalachians where you'll find one of the deepest canyons in the eastern United States.

Focus Area: Ecosystems

- Why are certain species in some environments but not in others?
- How do plants and animals rely on each other in an ecosystem?

 2 KATHY STILES FREELAND BIBB COUNTY GLADES PRESERVE

Nestled in the southern part of the Ridge and Valley ecoregion are outcrops of gray, prehistoric rock — and a botanical discovery for the ages.

Focus Area: Plant Identification

- Why can only some plants grow when dolomite is present?
- What physical characteristics of a plant can be used to identify it?

 3 SPLINTER HILL BOG

In the midst of Alabama's biggest ecoregion, the Southeastern Coastal Plain, is a pine-seepage bog where you'll find plants that are a bug's worst nightmare.

Focus Area: Fire Ecology and Carnivorous Plants

- What would happen if there were no fire in the longleaf pine ecosystem?
- How have carnivorous plants adapted to their environment?

WHO STUDIES ECOSYSTEMS? Have you ever seen a bird get nectar from a flower or an insect get caught in a spiderweb? Meet a type of scientist who studies plant and animal interactions, the kinds of relationships you'll learn about throughout this book.

 FIELD EXPERT **ECOLOGIST** Studies how organisms interact with one another and with their physical environment.

HOW ARE ECOSYSTEMS ORGANIZED? Your neighborhood may be organized into a hierarchy: individual families make up houses, houses make up a whole neighborhood, and your neighborhood plus other area neighborhoods make up an entire town.

Similarly, ecologists also organize ecosystems from simple to increasingly complex components. Studying the ecosystem at any one level allows them to see how human actions affect the environment.

Explore Further: learn the differences between these components. See "Ecology Levels," page 42.

1
LITTLE RIVER CANYON NATIONAL PRESERVE

LITTLE R.

COOSA R.

CAHABA R.

2
KATHY STILES FREELAND BIBB COUNTY GLADES PRESERVE

ALABAMA R.

3
SPLINTER HILL BOG

MOBILE BAY

THE UNDERWATER FOREST

TYPES OF PLACES YOU'LL EXPLORE:

1. Canyon
A narrow valley with steep walls. Canyons form over millions of years from a process called erosion where weather or a body of water will eventually wear away the land.

2. Ketona dolomite glade
A grassy opening within a woodland. This particular glade features rocky outcrops of the unusually pure ketona dolomite. Only certain plants can tolerate the high mineral content of the surrounding soils.

3. Bog
A type of peat-forming wetland that receives the majority of its water and nutrients from rain.

Around the time that humans were migrating out of Africa some 60,000 years ago, there stood a giant forest of cypress trees. It took a monster storm in 2004 to uncover this hidden natural treasure.

LITTLE RIVER CANYON
NATIONAL PRESERVE

LITTLE RIVER FALLS

ESTABLISHED
1992

SIZE
15,288 acres
stretching for 18 miles

MANAGED BY
National Park Service

VIDEO RESOURCE *Something About Little River*, a film that explores what a wild and scenic federal designation would mean to the local communities • From Southern Exposure and filmmaker Jeb Brackner ● vimeo.com/359702158

WATCH

LITTLE RIVER FALLS

CANYON VIEW OVERLOOK

GRACE'S HIGH FALLS

"THE GRAND CANYON OF THE EAST"

After many millennia, the Little River carved its way through eroding sandstone to create one of the most spectacular canyons east of the Mississippi River. From bogs to mixed pine forests, the preserve has an abundance of diverse wildlife.

DID YOU KNOW?

The Little River is the only river in the U.S. to flow atop a mountain.

Grace's High Falls is the state's tallest waterfall at 133 feet.

HIGHLIGHTS

The preserve has 18 naturally occurring plant communities (abbreviated list below), each with specific needs for light, food, and soil from their particular ecosystem.

Black Gum
Nyssa sylvatica

This tree prefers rich, moist soils, so it's only found in certain areas of the preserve (see bolded text below).

- Alabama Cumberland Sandstone Glade
- **Cumberland Forest Acidic Seep**
- **Eastern Gammagrass Shrubland**
- **Low Mountain Seepage Bog**
- Mixed Pine and Blueberry Forest
- Piedmont Beech / Heath Bluff
- **Sweetgum Floodplain Forest**

SIGHT

Odocoileus virginianus

Plunging down steep, nearly vertical canyon walls, the Little River weaves its way past gently sloping seepage bogs, outcrops of sandstone, and other rare plant habitats. **White-Tailed deer** forage for shrubs, wary of any predators like coyotes that may be lurking nearby.

SOUND

Two river otters purr and squeal as they chase each other through the water, while soaring in the skies above comes the guttural hiss of the **turkey vulture** on the hunt for dead flesh.

Cathartes aura

SMELL

The aggressive cottonmouth, a venomous blackish-brown snake with a triangular head and slit-shaped pupils, uses its strong sense of smell by flicking its tongue to "catch" scent molecules in the air.

TOUCH

The bushy, ring-tailed raccoon has a tactile advantage. Resembling human hands, its highly developed forepaws allow it to control prey and climb easily.

TASTE

The slithering snake attacks a **Fowler's toad**! But, the olive green amphibian defends itself by discharging a toxic secretion from the warts on its back, irritating the viper's mouth.

Anaxyrus fowleri

LITTLE RIVER CANYON
NATIONAL PRESERVE

Ecosystems are always undergoing changes in climate and availability of resources, but *EXTERNAL THREATS* like pollution and the presence of invasive species can make it even more difficult for plants and animals to adapt.

INVASIVE PLANTS

Plants that are native species naturally occur in a given geographic area. Invasive plants are introduced species outside their natural habitat that are often spread unknowingly by humans. These "alien" plants can outcompete native species for food because the insects and diseases of their new home don't affect them. This outcome disrupts the food chain because a decline in native plants also affects the animals that depend on them.

Find 4 in the illustration.
Japanese Stiltgrass
Microstegium vimineum

Find 3 in the illustration.
Chinese Privet
Ligustrum sinense

Find 2 in the illustration.
Japanese Honeysuckle
Lonicera japonica

ENERGY FLOW Because all living things must have energy to survive, species become interdependent upon one another. This transfer of energy can be described in the food chain, or the flow of energy and nutrients from one organism to another.

For example, the animals on the right all eat different things and can be grouped based on what they eat. **What part of the food chain does each fall under?** See "Ecosystem Interactions," page 43, to find out.

See "Ecosystem Interactions," page 43, to find out.

10

AT-RISK ECOSYSTEMS

Southern Appalachian Low Mountain Seepage Bog G1

Typically open, mostly treeless wetland areas found on or near the summit of Lookout Mountain.

Green Pitcher Plant G2
Sarracenia oreophila

Cinnamon Fern S
Osmunda cinnamomea

Nuttall's Lobelia S
Lobelia nuttallii

Eastern Gamagrass Shrubland G1

Areas prone to flooding, so trees and shrubs are typically stunted.

Eastern Gamagrass S
Tripsacum dactyloides

Common Buttonbush S
Cephalanthus occidentalis

Mountain Laurel S
Kalmia latifolia

St. John's Wort S
Hypericum densiflorum

Alabama Cumberland Sandstone Glade G2

Area characteristic of sandstone outcrops with shallow, acidic soils bordering dry woodlands.

Little River Onion G2
Allium speculae

Eastern Prickly Pear S
Opuntia humifusa

Menges' Fameflower G3
Phemeranthus mengesii

ANIMALS

Find 4 in the illustration.
Northern Flickers S
Colaptes auratus
Omnivore: insects, seeds

Find 2 in the illustration.
Turkey Vultures S
Cathartes aura
Carnivore: carrion

Find 3 in the illustration.
White-Tailed Deer S
Odocoileus virginianus
Herbivore: plants

Find 1 in the illustration.
Fowler's Toad S
Anaxyrus fowleri
Carnivore: insects, snails

Hidden Objects

Referring to page 10:

1 View the section "**Invasive Plants.**" Find and circle the number of species in the illustration.

2 View the section "**At-risk Ecosystems.**" Identify these areas in the illustration.

3 View the section "**Animals.**" Find and circle the number of species in the illustration.

Answer Key on page 41.

KATHY STILES FREELAND
BIBB COUNTY GLADES
PRESERVE

KETONA DOLOMITE

ESTABLISHED	SIZE	MANAGED BY
1996	480 acres	The Nature Conservancy, Alabama

LITTLE
CAHABA
RIVER

HIGHLIGHTS

The preserve hosts 61 rare plant species.

In the Cahaba River and its tributaries, 128 fish species occur, the most of any other river its size in the U.S.

Source: The Cahaba River Society
🌐 cahabariversociety.org

DID YOU KNOW?

Ketona dolomite occurred in the Cambrian geologic period, aging it from 500 to 544 million years old!

A BARREN ENVIRONMENT The dolomite found in Bibb County is unique because it is without the usual impurities that dilute other rock. Rich in magnesium, and surrounded by dry soils, it takes a certain type of plant to tolerate these conditions.

What's the difference between rocks and minerals, and how do scientists describe the age of rocks?
See "Geology," page 44.

FIELD EXPERT
GEOLOGIST Studies the structure and history of Earth as recorded in rocks.

"A BOTANICAL LOST WORLD"

In 1992, a canoe trip down the picturesque Cahaba River led botanist Jim Allison and friend Timothy Stevens to discover five species and three varieties of plants not seen anywhere else. It was remarkable to have uncovered so many new species in one area!

Solanum pumilum

SIGHT

Imagine a gently sloping, sparsely forested terrain with trees like red cedar and chinquapin oak. The open space is dotted with outcrops of blackish-gray dolomite and pockets of dwarf horse-nettle, a fragrant, star-shaped beauty that was once thought to be extinct and is now only found in Alabama.

Vaejovis carolinianus

TOUCH

The devil is on the loose! Favoring a more humid climate, the undersized southern devil scorpion stings its prey using the tip of its tail and then uses its pincers to grab and pull prey apart.

TASTE

The thimble-shaped candyroot has a secret that's hidden underground. Its root tastes like licorice when chewed.

Polygala nana

SOUND

Considered a pest by many a gardener, the eastern lubber grasshopper, a large and bold-patterned insect, puts on quite a show when disturbed. It will spread its wings, hiss, and expel air from its body, secreting a foul-smelling froth.

SMELL

13

KATHY STILES FREELAND
BIBB COUNTY GLADES
PRESERVE

Want to become competent at recognizing flowers? The table on the right lists a few descriptive plant traits that can be useful for identifying different species.

FLOWER VARIETY Just as humans are born with blond or black hair, feature blue or brown eyes, or wear a red or green hat, flowers also come in many different shapes, colors, and sizes.

Since their main function is to make seeds, flowers that do not self-pollinate will need the help of pollinators like birds, bats, bees, and other insects to reproduce. This occurs when pollen is transferred from the male anther to the female stigma.

THE PARTS OF A FLOWER

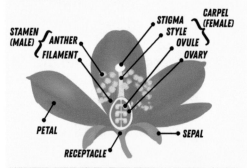

Learn about pollination: U.S. Forest Service,
🌐 https://bit.ly/3i4Uzff

FIELD EXPERT
BOTANIST Studies many aspects of plants and fungi. **Why?** Plants are essential to the survival of other species as they provide food, medicine, fuel, and other crucial needs.

PLANT IDENTIFICATION KEY

Flower Symmetry (Labeled "Symm." in worksheet)
Can the flower be divided into a mirror image of itself?

 ○ **Radial** Can the flower be divided into 3 or more identical parts? *Botany term: Actinomorphic*

 ○ **Bilateral** Can the flower only be divided in 1 plane? *Botany term: Zygomorphic*

 ○ **Asymmetrical** Does the flower lack any kind of symmetry?

Color (Choose all that apply.)

○ White   ○ Yellow   ○ Violet
○ Red   ○ Green   ○ Pink
○ Orange   ○ Blue   ○ Brown

Leaf Shape

 ○ **Linear**
Is the leaf long and narrow like a blade of grass?

 ○ **Oval-shaped**
Is the widest part of the leaf in the middle with ends that narrow equally?
Botany term: Elliptic

 ○ **Egg-shaped**
Is the leaf broader at the bottom with a tipping point?
Botany term: Ovate

 ○ **Spoon-shaped**
Is the top of the leaf broadly rounded, gradually getting narrower toward the stem?
Botany term: Spatulate

 ○ **Lance-shaped**
Is the leaf long and wide in the middle with a pointed tip?
Botany term: Lanceolate

Leaf Arrangement (Labeled "Arr." in worksheet)
How are the leaves arranged?

○ Alternate   ○ Opposite   ○ Basal

Plant Identification Worksheet

Look at each of the flowers and fill in the missing details using the plant identification key on page 14. Entries for **A** have been filled out for you.

Answer Key on page 41.

A Cahaba Indian Paintbrush G2
Castilleja kraliana

Family	
Figwort, *Scrophulariaceae*	
Symm.	Bilateral
Color	Yellow
Shape	Spoon-shaped
Arr.	Alternate

B Alabama Marbleseed G2
Onosmodium decipiens

Family	
Borage, *Boraginaceae*	
Symm.	
Color	
Shape	
Arr.	

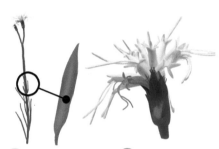

C Cahaba Torch G1
Liatris oligocephala

Family	
Aster, *Asteraceae*	
Symm.	
Color	
Shape	
Arr.	

D Ketona Tickseed S2
Coreopsis grandiflora var. inclinata

Family	
Aster, *Asteraceae*	
Symm.	
Color	
Shape	
Arr.	

E Cahaba Daisy Fleabane S2
Erigeron strigosus var. dolomiticola

Family	
Aster, *Asteraceae*	
Symm.	
Color	
Shape	
Arr.	

F Cahaba Prairie Clover G2
Dalea cahaba

Family	
Bean, *Fabaceae*	
Symm.	
Color	
Shape	
Arr.	

G Sticky Rosinwood G2
Silphium glutinosum

Family	
Aster, *Asteraceae*	
Symm.	
Color	
Shape	
Arr.	

H Alabama Pinkroot G2
Spigelia alabamensis

Family	
Logania, *Loganiaceae*	
Symm.	
Color	
Shape	
Arr.	

SPLINTER HILL BOG

LONGLEAF PINE &
WHITE-TOPPED PITCHER PLANTS

ESTABLISHED
2003, 2004

SIZE
2,100 acres

MANAGED BY
The Nature Conservancy and Forever
Wild Land Trust (FWLT) along with
the Alabama State Lands Division,
which manages two land tracts.

HIGHLIGHTS

Splinter Hill hosts 12 species of carnivorous plants including pitcher plants, sundews, and butterworts.

DID YOU KNOW?

A bog is not a swamp. Splinter Hill is known as a pine-seepage bog, a habitat consisting of longleaf pines that grow in poor, sandy soils. A bog can appear to be dry, but it is wet and spongy when walked upon.

FIELD EXPERT

FIRE ECOLOGIST Focuses on the origins of wildland fire and its relationship to the environment. Fire ecologists study how controlled fires can be used to maintain ecosystem health.

VIDEO RESOURCE

Secrets of the Longleaf Pine, a film about the role of fire in a resilient ecosystem
From AWR Studio
🌐 https://bit.ly/3eX3m14

WATCH

A LAND OF PREDATORS

Splinter Hill Bog thrives because of fire. Fire-causing lightning is Earth's natural strategy for healthy forests, but long before the arrival of European settlers, Native Americans prescribed fire to kickstart new plant growth. They knew that without a periodic disturbance like fire, dense vines and shrubs would dominate the understory and prevent light from reaching other plants — thereby limiting the Native Americans' food resources.

SIGHT In the midst of this fire-dependent landscape, there is a tree whose superpower allows it to survive fire: the longleaf pine. This king of the savanna, reaches heights of up to 100 feet!

TASTE If you're feeling brave, chewing the root of **toothache grass** will make your mouth go numb!

Ctenium aromaticum

TOUCH The simple beauty of the bright **yellow butterwort** is not so innocent. The leaves of this predatory plant are covered with sticky droplets that help it trap insects for its next meal!

Pinguicula lutea

SOUND There's a buzz in the air, but take a closer look. Though the **greater bee fly** may resemble and act like a bumblebee, it has only one pair of wings, while bees have two. This furry parasite mimics the bee in order to gain access to its host's nest.

SMELL As its name suggests, when the wilting leaves of **vanillaleaf** are crushed, it emits a sweet, vanilla-like scent.

Bombylius major

Carphephorus odoratissimus

17

SPLINTER HILL BOG

NOTABLE PLANT AND ANIMAL SPECIES

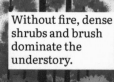
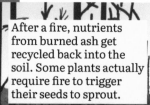

Without fire, dense shrubs and brush dominate the understory.

After a fire, nutrients from burned ash get recycled back into the soil. Some plants actually require fire to trigger their seeds to sprout.

Longleaf seedlings and grasses have the space and sunlight they need to grow once the competing plants are gone.

Many wildlife species have evolved to live with fire. The gopher tortoise uses its burrows to escape fire, along with many other species that depend on these underground tunnels.

A. Gopher Tortoise G3
Gopherus polyphemus
Family: Tortoise, *Testudinidae*

THE ECOSYSTEM ENGINEER
💬 *I have shovel-like front legs for digging underground burrows that over 350 species rely on as a shelter or food source. This makes me a keystone species.*

B. Black Pine Snake S2
Pituophis melanoleucus lodingi
Family: Snake, *Colubridae*

SERPENT OF THE SAVANNA
💬 *I can cover some territory – my home range is about 117 acres where I will use gopher tortoise burrows to hunt for small rodents. If you disturb me, I will hiss loudly, vibrate my tail, and strike repeatedly! Lucky for you, I am non-venomous.*

C. Pitcher Plant Mining Moth G3
Exyra semicrocea
Family: Owlet Moths, *Noctuidae*

PITCHER PLANT INFILTRATOR
💬 *I have specially adapted claws that allow me to navigate a pitcher plant's interior surfaces without becoming trapped!*

D. American Chaffseed S1
Schwalbea americana
Family: Figworts, *Scrophulariaceae*

THE FIRE-LOVING FLOWER
💬 *I am a half parasite, so although I undergo photosynthesis, I must extract other nutrients from the root of my host. Like pitcher plants, I need fire to regenerate stem growth.*

E. Bachman's Sparrow G3
Peucaea aestivalis
Family: Bunting, *Emberizidae*

SECRETIVE SPARROW
💬 *Birdwatchers look for me, but I am elusive! As a ground forager, I prefer to build my nests at the base of shrubs or in clumps of grass. I escape predators by hiding in tortoise burrows.*

F. Pine Woods Treefrog S
Hyla femoralis
Family: Treefrog, *Hylidae*

THE "MORSE CODE" FROG
💬 *My distinctive call is like saying "getta" rapidly. Typically arboreal, I can climb high into the longleaf pine where tasty insects like spiders and ants hide under thick bark.*

Color the pitcher plants.

Then draw your own and include any insects it might eat.

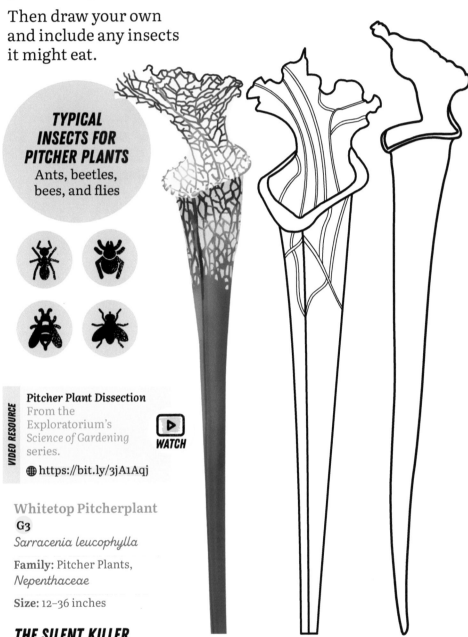

TYPICAL INSECTS FOR PITCHER PLANTS
Ants, beetles, bees, and flies

VIDEO RESOURCE

Pitcher Plant Dissection
From the Exploratorium's *Science of Gardening* series.

WATCH

🌐 https://bit.ly/3jA1Aqj

Whitetop Pitcherplant
G3
Sarracenia leucophylla

Family: Pitcher Plants, *Nepenthaceae*

Size: 12–36 inches

THE SILENT KILLER

💬 *The soils I live in are typically nutrient-poor, so I must find energy in other ways. As a carnivorous plant, I have a secret weapon — my tubular shape acts as a pitfall trap! I have a sweet-smelling nectar that lures insects to me. Once inside, they are unable to escape the downward-facing hairs lining my tube. As the insects fall to the bottom, I have special digestive fluids that convert them into the nutrients that will give me energy.*

Ecosystem Threats
Fire suppression, conversion of habitat to pine plantations

WATER

132K
MILES OF RIVER AND STREAM CHANNELS

3.6M
ACRES OF WETLAND

563K
ACRES OF PONDS, LAKES, AND RESERVOIRS

DID YOU KNOW?

Alabama leads the U.S. in the following aquatic species:

97 SPECIES OF CRAYFISH
Coosa Crayfish
Cambarus coosae
FOUND IN COOSA RIVER SYSTEM

181 SPECIES OF MUSSELS
Pink Mucket
Lampsilis abrupta
FOUND IN TENNESSEE RIVER SYSTEM

204 SPECIES OF SNAILS
Spotted Rocksnail
Leptoxis picta
FOUND IN ALABAMA RIVER SYSTEM

280 SPECIES OF FRESHWATER FISH
Blue Shiner
Cyprinella caerulea
FOUND IN COOSA RIVER SYSTEM

Sources: Alabama Rivers Alliance, 🌐 alabamarivers.org • Alabama Rivers and Streams Network 🌐 alh2o.org

MAJOR RIVERS

TENNESSEE R. • FLINT R. • PAINT ROCK R. • TENNESSEE R. • LITTLE R. • BEAR CRK. • SIPSEY FORK • MULBERRY FORK • LOCUST FORK • COOSA R. • TERRAPIN CRK. • LITTLE TALLAPOOSA • BUTTAHATCHEE CRK. • SIPSEY RIVER • BLACK WARRIOR R. • CAHABA R. • WEOGUFKA CRK. • HATCHET CRK. • TALLAPOOSA R. • CHATTAHOOCHEE R. • TOMBIGBEE R. • AUTAUGA CRK. • SUCARNOOCHEE R. • ALABAMA R. • TOMBIGBEE R. • ALABAMA R. • PATSALIGA CRK. • PEA R. • CHOCTAWHATCHEE R. • ESCATAWPA R. • TENSAW R. • ESCAMBIA R. • SEPULGA R. • CONECUH R. • YELLOW R. • MOBILE R. • MOBILE BAY

5 Rivers Delta
Blakeley River
Apalachee River
Tensaw River
Spanish River
Mobile River

Longest River:
Tennessee River at 652 miles

Wild & Scenic River Designation:
Sipsey Fork of the West Fork River,
Wild: 36.4 miles, Scenic: 25 miles, Total: 61.4 miles

Source: National Wild & Scenic Rivers System 🌐 rivers.gov

Alabama is unrivaled when it comes to aquatic species diversity. And nowhere is this more apparent than in the Mobile-Tensaw River Bottomlands (see also page 33), an area covering 260,000 acres, making it the second largest delta in the United States. Other than hosting 120 species of aquatic snails, this is the only place you'll find the rare red-bellied turtle.

NOTABLE AQUATIC AND SEMIAQUATIC SPECIES

Alabama Heelsplitter G3
Lasmigona alabamensis
Family: River mussels, *Unionidae*

Alabama Sturgeon G1
Scaphirhynchus suttkusi
Family: Sturgeon, *Acipenseridae*

Gulf Saltmarsh Snake S2
Nerodia clarkii clarkii
Family: Colubrid, *Colubridae*

STATE REPTILE
Alabama Red-Bellied Turtle G1
Pseudemys alabamensis
Family: Pond turtles, *Emydidae*

STATE SALTWATER FISH
(Fighting) Tarpon S
Megalops atlanticus
Family: Oxeye herring, *Megalopidae*

STATE FRESHWATER FISH
Largemouth Bass S
Micropterus salmoides
Family: Sunfish, *Centrarchidae*

💬 What Species Am I?

Match the descriptions below with the correct animal.

Answer Key on page 41.

_____ Alabama Heelsplitter   _____ Alabama Sturgeon   _____ Gulf Saltmarsh Snake

_____ Alabama Red-Bellied
        Turtle   _____ (Fighting) Tarpon   _____ Largemouth Bass

A *Known as the "silver king," I can grow up to 8 feet! I prefer warm, shallow coastal waters but can also travel upriver into fresh water. I like to eat fish, crab, and shrimp and am highly regarded for my fighting ability.*

B *A golden blur, I move along the river bottoms of deep, fast-moving channels using my whiskers to locate crustaceans to eat. At an average length of 30 inches, I was once sold commercially, but now I am rarely ever found.*

C *I eat only plants – that makes me an herbivore. My average length is 12–15 inches, and you can find me in shallow waters of freshwater streams and rivers. I am named for a colorful, defining feature of my body.*

D *At 5.5 inches, I like to burrow at the bottom of freshwater streams, pumping water to obtain food and oxygen. I get my name from the pain I can cause if stepped on with bare feet.*

E *Sometimes called "Ol' Bucketmouth," I'm able to eat small fish, crayfish, frogs, and even mice! I can be found in lakes and rivers and have an average length of 17 inches.*

F *If you dare, you can find my striped body in estuaries and tidal mud flats, though I am good at hiding among the seaweed or in crab burrows. Reaching up to 20 inches, I devour small fish, crab, and shrimp.*

WATER

Alabama Red-Bellied Turtle G1
Pseudemys alabamensis

Family: Pond Turtles, *Emydidae*

Size: 12–15 inches

Geographic Range: Mobile and Baldwin counties

Habitat: Sandy bottoms of shallow, freshwater streams and rivers and slightly salty water of bays and bayous

Food Habits: Aquatic plants

Predators: Fish crows, raccoons, alligators, shore birds, snakes, mammals

Ecosystem Threats: Loss of suitable nesting areas, illegal trapping, used as food for humans, and more

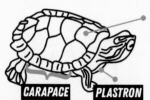

SCUTES
A thickened horny or bony plate on a turtle's shell

CARAPACE   PLASTRON

BIRMINGHAM

MOBILE

RED-BELLIED DARLING OF THE DELTA

HIGHLIGHTS

Named for the pale yellow and orange to red plastron (underside of shell) and featuring a brownish to black carapace (outer shell).

Has a notch at the tip of its upper jaw, a distinctive feature of this species.

Has a life expectancy of 50 years.

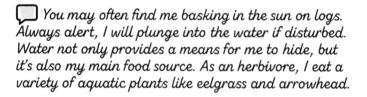 *You may often find me basking in the sun on logs. Always alert, I will plunge into the water if disturbed. Water not only provides a means for me to hide, but it's also my main food source. As an herbivore, I eat a variety of aquatic plants like eelgrass and arrowhead.*

Alabama Sturgeon (G1)
Scaphirhynchus suttkusi

Family: Sturgeon, *Acipenseridae*

Size: 30 inches and 2–3 pounds

Current Geographic Range: Lower Cahaba and Alabama rivers

Habitat: Swift-moving channels of major rivers

Food Habits: Larval aquatic insects, mollusks, fish eggs, and fish

Ecosystem Threats: Habitat loss, siltation, water degradation, overfishing, hydroelectric dams, and more

ENVIRONMENTAL DNA is DNA collected from environmental samples like soil or seawater rather than directly from the organism.

Learn about e-DNA: U.S. Geological Survey
🌐 https://on.doi.gov/2ZVXIIE

— Historical range
— Current range

THE GOLDEN GHOST

HIGHLIGHTS

Features a distinctive yellowish-orange hue.

A migratory fish that swims upstream to spawn so that larvae can drift downstream to develop into adults.

Sturgeon in general are collected for caviar (fish eggs), which impacts their population numbers.

💬 *I once roamed in a thousand-mile range that included many major river systems, but overfishing and other threats have reduced my river habitat to just 152 miles of the Alabama and lower Cahaba rivers.*

It has been a decade since I was last observed, and biologists can only speculate that I still exist. They use Environmental DNA (e-DNA), a monitoring tool that has found traces of me in the rivers. With more barrier-free passages to allow me to swim upstream, maybe I could make a comeback. There's still so much to learn about me!

PLANT

~3K NATIVE PLANT SPECIES

29 ENDEMIC SPECIES

Source: Alabama Plant Atlas
🌐 floraofalabama.org

STATE TREE
Longleaf Pine Ⓢ
Pinus palustris

Family: Pine, *Pinaceae*

Size: 100–120 feet

KING OF THE SAVANNA

💬 *I am an evergreen conifer with a life span that stretches through centuries! My seeds, the largest of all southern pines, develop within cones where the wind disperses them to the ground to germinate. Fire is essential to my survival as it helps clear leaf litter. If the seeds cannot reach the ground, then other trees like hardwoods and southern pines would take over — and they already have. I once dominated North America, covering almost 90 million acres. Sadly, my range is now reduced to a mere 3.4 million acres, affecting hundreds of plant and animal species that rely on my ecosystem.*

Source: American Forests,
🌐 americanforests.org

ALABAMA'S NATIVE PLANT COMMUNITIES

UPLANDS

FALL LINE

LOWLANDS

More than 60 million years ago, during the Cretaceous Period, ancient seas carved a geographic boundary called the Fall Line. Some species of plants live all over the state, while other species live either north or south of the line due to differences in climate patterns, soil types, and other environmental factors.

Map Source: Auburn University, Donald E. Davis Arboretum
🌐 https://bit.ly/32OtLdy

 Coastal Dunes

 Maritime Hammock

 Coastal Pitcher Plant Bogs

 Long Leaf Pines

 Black Belt Prairies

 Sandstone Outcrops

 Ketona Glades

 Montane Long Leaf Pines

 Mountain Bog

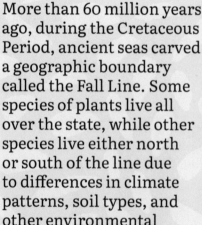

STATE WILDFLOWER
Oak Leaf Hydrangea Ⓢ
Hydrangea quercifolia

Family: Hydrangea,
Hydrangeaceae

Size: 4–8 foot shrub

STATE INSECT
Monarch Butterfly Ⓢ
Danaus plexippus

Family: Brush-footed
Butterflies, *Nymphalidae*

Size: 4-inch wingspan

Color the wildflowers.

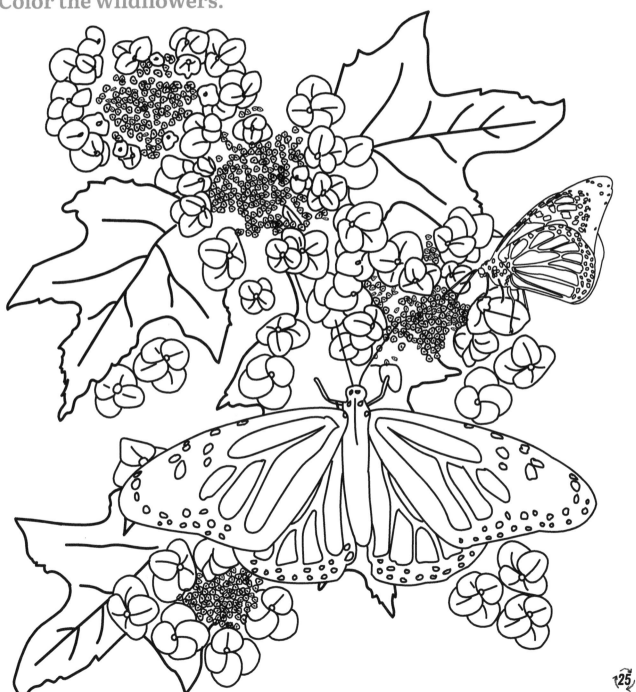

PLANT

ALABAMA'S UNDERWATER FOREST

~60,000 years ago

PREHISTORIC TIMELINE

~45,000 years ago

A. A grove of behemoth-sized cypress trees, some as big as 30 feet in diameter, once reigned over their primeval domain.
B. Environmental conditions were unstable during this time. Sea levels increased and decreased repeatedly over thousands of years. **C.** Eventually, the Gulf waters submerged the trees entirely, burying them in layers of sediment and mud, which provided an airtight barrier against the sea water. Since there is no oxygen underwater, the trees remain preserved.

A MUCH COOLER CLIMATE

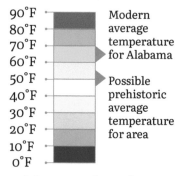

90°F
80°F
70°F
60°F → Modern average temperature for Alabama
50°F
40°F → Possible prehistoric average temperature for area
30°F
20°F
10°F
0°F

Earth has experienced multiple ice ages, which occur every 40 to 100,000 years. During an ice age dating 60,000 years ago, temperatures were not only cooler but scientists estimate that sea levels were about 400 feet lower than today because most water was in glacier form.

26

A CLIMATIC EVENT

Since trees are sensitive to temperature and moisture, the thickness of their rings can reveal weather patterns for every year of their life. When scientists matched up the grains of wood samples, tree ring data showed periods of stress and growth and finally that all the trees died at the same time. Since bald cypress trees will die if exposed to salt water, scientists speculate the trees drowned from rising sea levels.

WHAT THE DIRT REVEALS

Scientists were surprised to find a layer of peat in the ocean floor, an organic material typically found in a swamp or bog rather than the Gulf area. Pollen in this layer helped determine that the underwater forest was meant for a colder place like the coastal forests of North or South Carolina.

SEDIMENT LAYERS
- Holocene sand
- Sand and marine clay
- Peat

FIELD EXPERTS

A *DENDROCHRONOLOGIST* studies climate conditions and past events by analyzing the growth of tree rings.

A *PALYNOLOGIST* studies living or fossilized plant spores and pollen grains to recreate past environments.

2004

2012

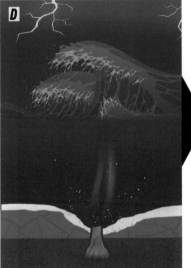 

D. Hurricane Ivan, a Category 5 storm, ravaged the coast of Alabama in 2004. Scientists believe the intense 140-mph winds and massive, 98-foot waves uncovered the sediment that kept the trees hidden. **E.** In 2012, teams of scientists began numerous studies of the underwater forest. As a natural archive, it was a rare opportunity to understand the effects of long-term climate change.

HOW OLD IS THE FOREST?

To determine the age of the forest, scientists first tried radiocarbon dating, but those methods suggested the trees were much older than the testing could account for (radiocarbon dating can go up to 50,000 years). So, a team of geologists took samples of the sediment using a vibracore machine, a tool that traps dirt particles by inserting a metal tube into the sea floor. By measuring layers of sediment from where various wood samples were found, the researchers determined the trees to be between 50,000 and 60,000 years old! Steps are being taken to protect the forest as a national marine sanctuary, as it is like no other place on the planet.

VIDEO RESOURCE

The Underwater Forest, a documentary detailing the discovery and exploration of this ancient cypress forest Presented by "This is Alabama," written and directed by Ben Raines ⊕ thisisalabama.org/underwaterforest

▶ **WATCH**

A *PALEONTOLOGIST* studies the history of life on Earth based on fossils.

A *PALEOCLIMATOLOGIST* studies the climate of past ages, reconstructing conditions based on the evidence they find in the geologic record like glacial deposits, fossils, and sediments.

Bald Cypress Ⓢ
Taxodium distichum

Family: Cypress, *Cupressaceae*

Size:
35–120 feet

ANCIENT SENTINEL OF THE SOUTH

💬 *They call me bald because, though I am cone-bearing, I shed my needles as it gets colder. Hardy and tough, I can adapt to various soil types, whether dry, wet, or swampy, with the extra support of "knees" developed from my root system. I'm important to the ecosystem because I help reduce flood damage, and my canopy provides nesting sites for a variety of birds.*

AL

MOBILE BAY

UNDERWATER FOREST

ICE AGE COASTLINE 12,000 TO 18,000 YEARS AGO

CLUES TO THE FUTURE?

The substantial wetland we know as Mobile Bay was once a forested valley with an ancient river carving its way to the sea. All that remains of that prehistoric wonderland are the stumps of giant trees still rooted into the seafloor. It takes a team of specialized scientists to unlock the clues this forest holds, and what they discover could tell us a lot about how environments respond to climate change and rising sea levels — and what that could mean for our own future.

ANIMAL

62 NATIVE MAMMAL SPECIES INCLUDING:

	22	species of rodents
	16	species of bats
	11	species of carnivores
	6	species of insectivores
	4	species of rabbits
	1	ungulate
	1	opossum
	1	armadillo

Source: Outdoor Alabama 🌐 outdooralabama.com

STATE MAMMAL
American Black Bear Ⓢ
Ursus americanus

Family: Bears, *Ursidae*

Size: 4–7 feet

THE ALABAMA RAMBLER
💬 *You've probably heard about me – I am the most common bear in North America. Do you know that I'm solitary, curious, and highly territorial? Oh, and I love to sleep! Once I hibernate, my metabolism slows down, and I can go hundreds of days without eating, drinking, peeing, or pooping!*

STATE BIRD
Northern Flicker Ⓢ
Colaptes auratus

Family: Woodpeckers, *Picidae*

Size: 11–13 inches

THE "YELLOWHAMMER"
💬 *Nicknamed for my yellow underwings, I'm unlike other woodpeckers in that I have a weak beak. I make up for it with a long, barbed tongue used to scoop up large amounts of ants at a time!*

A FEW OF ALABAMA'S ENDEMIC SPECIES

There are some species you can't find anywhere else outside of Alabama. They are truly special!

A. Manitou Cavesnail Ⓖ1
Antrorbis breweri

Family: Mud Snails, *Hydrobiidae*

Size: 2.7–3 milimeters

B. Black Warrior Waterdog Ⓖ1
Necturus alabamensis

Family: Waterdogs, *Proteidae Bonaparte*

Size: 6–8 inches

C. Watercress Darter Ⓖ1
Etheostoma nuchale

Family: Perches, *Percidae*

Size: 2.5-inches avg. length

D. Red Hills Salamander Ⓖ2
Phaeognathus hubrichti

Family: Lungless salamanders, *Plethodontidae*

Size: up to 11 inches

E. Alabama Beach Deermouse Ⓢ1
Peromyscus polionotus ammobates

Family New World rats and mice, *Cricetidae*

Size: 4–5 inches

```
B W J Q W A T E R C R E S S D A R T E R
A O Y G J B F I G H T I N G T A R P O N
C G D B E L O I E K R U R O L E P O B W
H C R E L U R L P E D W Y P Q D L M H O
M C R A U A Y U D F U V F H I X H S E A
A R Q C Y B C B H O B L U E S H I N E R
N Q U H O B E K A W J A U R V C E L L C
S A T D R L A E B L N B L T V R E R S R
S T P E L H G T G E B T G D G B S S P E
P Z U E H J E Z M R A Z F R E S U B L S
A Y D R E A M Q L S U R J T Z A J G I S
R K C M G N C G N T E P W O L U G X T W
R I Z O N E U Q U O N L K I E R O L T A
O U P U S V O I N A R U E S G B T W E T
W Q T S L P L N T D I I H E L Z E E R T
E S T E R E D B E L L I E D T U R T L E
O I X V X F A C Q W N S T N P R I E M R
N O Z K K L A R G E M O U T H B A S S X
N O R T H E R N F L I C K E R T A N A U
N O M I R W P Z A W K R D U D I L S R W
```

Word Search

Find and circle all of the animals listed below. The hidden word can be positioned in all directions: horizontally, vertically, and diagonally. The word will always be written from left to right and on one straight line.

Answer Key on page 41.

Bachmans Sparrow

Bald Eagle

Beach Deermouse

Black Bear

Blue Shiner

Fighting Tarpon

Fowlers Toad

Gopher Tortoise

Heelsplitter

Largemouth Bass

Northern Flicker

Red Bellied Turtle

Sturgeon

Watercress Darter

ANIMAL

PROFILE
ALABAMA BEACH DEERMOUSE

Alabama Beach Deermouse **S1**
Peromyscus polionotus ammobates

Family: New World rats and mice, *Cricetidae*

Size: 4–5 inches including tail

Geographic Range: Ft. Morgan, Gulf State Park, Bon Secour National Wildlife Refuge

Habitat: Various types of sand dunes (primary, secondary, and scrub) with beach grass and shrub cover

Food Habits: Fruits and seeds of dune plants, acorns, and insects

Predators: Cats, snakes, owls, red foxes

Ecosystem Threats: Competition with house mice, commercial and residential development, roadway construction, hurricanes and tropical storms, exotic vegetation, and more

BIRMINGHAM

MOBILE

THE DUNE DWELLER

HIGHLIGHTS

Lives primarily in burrows, sometimes up to 10 per family, with each den consisting of an entrance, a nest chamber, and an escape route.

Nocturnal — forages for most of its food at night.

💬 *I am known as an indicator species because I help disperse the seeds that help vegetation like sea oats, bluestem, and evening primrose to grow. This is especially critical when tropical storms occur because these plants help stabilize the area by reducing the impact of wind and water on the dunes.*

Red Hills Salamander G2
Phaeognathus hubrichti

Family: Lungless salamanders, *Plethodontidae*

Size: up to 11 inches

Current Geographic Range: 6 counties comprising the Red Hills region of south-central Alabama, between the Alabama and Conecuh rivers

Habitat: Steep ridges and moist ravines that slope down into slow, shallow streams within mixed hardwood forests including magnolias, beech, oaks, and others

Food Habits: Crickets, spiders, earthworms, snails, mites, fly larvae

Predators: Birds, snakes, coyotes, badgers

Ecosystem Threats: Soil disturbance from logging, conversion of forest, and more

BIRMINGHAM

THE SUBTERRANEAN SALAMANDER

HIGHLIGHTS

Spends most of its time underground.

Has the ability to do a body-roll maneuver to make burrows bigger and to escape predators.

💬 *I may be one of the largest lungless salamanders, but you may never see me because I rarely leave my den and will defend it if threatened. With bared teeth, I propel myself forward and "head-butt" any intruders, hopefully knocking them out of the burrow. Of course, this only works when the intruder is the same size as me!*

CALL OF THE WILD

CONSERVING ALABAMA'S SPECIAL PLACES

SPECIES IN ALABAMA THAT ARE GONE

116

SPECIES PRESUMED EXTIRPATED (STATUS SX) IN ALABAMA:

 3 plants
 10 freshwater fishes
 5 birds
 92 mussels, snails
 6 mammals including:

American Bison
Bison bison

Gray Wolf
Canis lupus

Red Wolf
Canis rufus

Elk
Cervus elaphus

Cougar
Puma concolor

Florida Panther
Puma concolor coryi

NatureServe defines SX as "species not located despite intensive searches and virtually no likelihood of rediscovery."

SPECIES IN ALABAMA THAT ARE AT-RISK

143

ENDANGERED AND THREATENED SPECIES IN ALABAMA:

 23 plants
120 animals

Information subject to change. For current findings, visit the U.S. Fish & Wildlife Service at ⊕ fws.gov

Conservation is the prevention of a wasteful use of a resource.

Alabama has an abundance of plant and animal biodiversity, but it's also a state with some of the highest extinction rates in North America.

LIMIT PLASTIC POLLUTION One of the most obvious impacts on the environment by humans comes from food packaging. Plastic including bottles, bottle caps, and bags are a major concern to the health of forests and waterways. These one-time-use items can leach chemicals into waterways or be swallowed by aquatic species that transfer the bits of plastic up the food chain.

TAKING ACTION Check out Litter Quitters, an anti-litter video competition between public high schools in the Birmingham area. Students create promotional videos to raise awareness about the harm litter causes. Winners receive a cash prize for the most online votes through YouTube.

⊕ litterquitters.org

NATIONAL NATURAL LANDMARKS PROGRAM

National Natural Landmarks Program ⊕ nps.gov

Here are three highlights from the seven sites in Alabama that the National Park Service has designated as "the best remaining examples of specific biological and/or geological features":

Alabama Cave Shrimp **S1**
Palaemonias alabamae

1. Shelta Cave

4 acres • Private ownership

This 2,500-foot-long cave features an underground lake and is home to 24 cave-dependent species like the Alabama cave shrimp. This critically imperiled species has adapted to its dark world with a nearly transparent outer shell. Contamination of groundwater is the leading cause for its decline in population.

2. Dismals Canyon

85 acres • Private ownership

Amidst one of the last stands of virgin forest in this valley formed of sandstone rocks is a rare, bioluminescent species of fly found in North America known locally as a "dismalite." In its larval form, it will produce a blue light to attract flying prey into its sticky webs.

Water Tupelo Ⓢ
Nyssa aquatica

Family
Dogwood, Cornaceae

Size 50–100 feet

THE HONEYMAKER
💬 *Residing in the delta's murky swamps, I am a specially adapted tree that plays a critical role in the ecosystem because I purify water and absorb CO2. Bees and other wildlife love me as a source for food and shelter, and my flowers are known to produce a popular kind of honey.*

VIDEO RESOURCE

America's Amazon, a documentary about the biological richness of the delta
From Alabama Public Television Presents
🌐 https://bit.ly/39vlyhu

▶ WATCH

3. Mobile-Tensaw River Bottomlands

179,000 acres · Federal, State, Private ownership

This maze of waterways is Alabama's largest wetland, encompassing thousands of acres of habitat like tidal marshes, cypress-tupelo swamps, and bottomland forests.

How did this area come to be?
At the end of an ice age 10,000 years ago, global temperatures started to increase causing the glaciers to melt and sea waters to rise. The delta is an ancient valley now covered with water!

What wildlife lives here?

1,071 SPECIES IN THE DELTA   **67** SPECIES ARE RARE, IMPERILED, THREATENED, OR ENDANGERED IN THE DELTA

- 🌱 **500** plants
- 🐦 **300** birds
- 🐟 **126** fishes
- 🐻 **46** mammals
- 🐍 **69** reptiles
- 🦎 **30** amphibians

Information subject to change. For current findings, visit Outdoor Alabama 🌐 outdooralabama.com

Ecosystem Threats
The effects of human population growth and the toll of invasive species like feral hogs and fire ants are just some of the biggest factors for habitat loss in the delta.

Conservation Efforts
Some species like the ivory-billed woodpecker are no longer in Alabama, but cooperation by many local and government partners creates success stories like the recovery of the bald eagle.

EXTIRPATED
Ivory-Billed Woodpecker ⒼⰟ
Campephilus principalis

RECOVERED
Bald Eagle Ⓢ
Haliaeetus leucocephalus

RUN WILD!
SELF-GUIDED ACTIVITIES

CONSERVATION BEGINS WITH YOU!

Technology makes modern living easier for humans, and that's a good thing! But, as global citizens, we've made some choices that have disrupted and altered the environment in ways that could be irreversible.

While change in nature is inevitable, some species have specific needs for survival and may not always be able to adapt to a changing environment. Altering our behavior and taking more sustainable actions can reduce the rate of negative impact. Working together to safeguard our wild places now ensures that everyone can enjoy them in the future.

WE SHOULD CARE ABOUT CONSERVATION BECAUSE:

We are all interconnected.
As species compete for and share resources with each other, intricate relationships emerge. Remember the gopher tortoise? A decline in its population would affect some 350 other species who rely on its burrows. Every species is linked to a multitude of others in an ecosystem.

Species extinction is happening at an accelerated rate.
Scientists are calling this time period the "age of humans"— our impact on the natural world is causing species to become extinct at an alarming rate. Perhaps there's a plant that holds the next medical breakthrough or an animal that inspires a new invention. If humans continue at our current rate, we may never find out.

A starter list of ideas to practice sustainable living:

PLAY OUTSIDE AND EXPLORE!
Practice your observation skills. Take time to really look and see the things around you. Start a nature journal to keep track of what you see. Use the plant identification key on page 14 to hone your skills in plant recognition.

Explore this resource for journaling ideas 🌐 https://bit.ly/3jKeemS

RESPECT WILDLIFE
Admire animals from a distance, and avoid disturbing their homes. Don't pick wildflowers in vulnerable ecosystems. Practice Leave No Trace principles.

Learn more: National Park Service 🌐 https://bit.ly/3fVElF9

START A POLLINATOR GARDEN
Discuss with your family about creating a pollinator-friendly garden by planting native species.

Learn more: U.S. Forest Service 🌐 https://bit.ly/3j4XsoM

PARTICIPATE IN A COMMUNITY CLEAN-UP
Find and join a group near you that picks up litter from area lakes, rivers, beaches, and trails.

🌐 nationalcleanupday.org

SUPPORT ORGANIZATIONS THAT PROTECT OUR WILDLIFE
Consider raising money for or volunteering at a nearby nature center, local park, land trust, or wildlife agency.

Find a park: Discover the Forest 🌐 discovertheforest.org

What are some other ways you can think of to promote sustainable conservation practices?

Advocate for Alabama's Wildlife.

To advocate is to publicly support a cause.

1 Think about a story or issue from this book to use for your project.

One idea would be to create awareness for an endangered plant or animal. Questions on the right have been provided, or choose a topic of your own.

2 Choose how to execute your idea whether it's a poster, comic strip, magazine spread, or your own idea.

3 Learn more about your focus area.

For resources: go online, use local or school library resources, or talk to an expert from a local park.

4 Create your project in the space provided on pages 36–37.

5 Share what you know with someone else — this is how we can make positive change! Having knowledge about particular issues will help you and others to better understand how to protect Alabama's wildlife.

Submit your artwork to the Wild 50 States gallery! For more information, please visit: ⊕ wild50states.com/gallery-form

---

SPECIES NAME

_____

Describe the species' habitat.
Think about where it lives.

How does this species get its energy?
Think about where it fits in the food chain.

Describe any natural or human impacts on this species.
Are there invasive species, pollution, or impediments like dams?

What steps are being taken to protect it?

What interests you most about this species, and why do you think it's worth saving?

Continued on the next page.

Create your artwork here.

RUN WILD!
SELF-GUIDED ACTIVITIES

What habitat do you live in?

Find an outdoor place like your backyard, local park, or neighborhood.

To find your nearest outdoor park, go online at: ⊕ discovertheforest.org

1 **List** the physical features of your habitat below.

2 **Write** down your observations using the space on the right.

OBSERVATIONS

What animals and their interactions did you see? *What did they eat? Did they need to do anything to stay safe from other animals?*

What do your observations tell you about what living things need in order to survive? *Think about your home and what your own needs are and draw comparisons.*

Draw your habitat below:

Design your own species.

As a globe-trotting adventurer, you've discovered an amazing new species! Perhaps it's an animal that is a combination between a rabbit and a lizard, or a bizarre plant that has fangs. Use your imagination and have fun!

1 **Record** details of its description below.

Describe its habitat.

What does it eat?

What special features does it have?

2 **Draw** your new species in its habitat using the space on the right.

SPECIES NAME

_____

Submit your artwork to the Wild 50 States gallery! For more information, please visit: 🌐 wild50states.com/gallery-form

 39

GLOSSARY

abiotic · *noun*
A nonliving thing.

arboreal · *adjective*
Chiefly of animals living in trees.

bayou · *noun*
A body of water (as a creek) that flows slowly through marshy land.

biodiversity · *noun*
The variety of life in the world or in a particular habitat or ecosystem.

biotic · *noun*
A living thing.

carnivore · *noun*
(Of an animal) an organism that eats mostly meat, or the flesh of animals.

(Of a plant) an organism that traps and digests small animals, especially insects.

conifer · *noun*
A tree that bears cones and needle-like or scale-like leaves that are typically evergreen.

conservation · *noun*
Prevention of wasteful use of a resource.

delta · *noun*
A piece of land in the shape of a triangle or fan made by deposits of mud and sand at the mouth of a river.

dolomite · *noun*
A translucent mineral consisting of a carbonate of calcium and magnesium.

ecosystem · *noun*
Includes all of the living things (plants, animals, and organisms) in a given area, interacting with each other, and also with their nonliving environments (weather, earth, sun, soil, climate, atmosphere).

endemic · *adjective*
(A plant or animal) native and restricted to a certain place.

environment · *noun*
All of the biotic and abiotic factors that act on an organism, population, or ecological community and influence its survival and development.

estuary · *noun*
An area where seawater mixes with fresh water.

extirpated species · *noun*
A species or population that no longer exists within a certain geographical location.

fauna · *noun*
The animals of a particular region, habitat, or geological period.

flora · *noun*
The plants of a particular region, habitat, or geological period.

food chain · *noun*
The transfer of food energy from one organism to another in a particular environment.

fossil · *noun*
The remains of plants, animals, fungi, bacteria, and single-celled living things that have been replaced by rock material or impressions of organisms preserved in rock.

germinate · *verb*
(Of a seed or spore) to grow and put out shoots after a period of dormancy.

habitat · *noun*
Physical location of a community, population, and individuals.

herbivore · *noun*
An organism that feeds mostly on plants.

indicator species · *noun*
An organism that serves as a measure of the environmental conditions that exist in a given locale.

insectivore · *noun*
An organism that feeds mostly on insects.

interdependence · *noun*
The survival of species is dependent on other living organisms and nonliving components.

invasive species · *noun*
Organisms that are non-native (or alien) in a given region and whose introduction is likely to have a negative effect.

keystone species · *noun*
A species on which other species in an ecosystem largely depend, such that if it were removed, the ecosystem would change drastically.

mammal · *noun*
An animal that breathes air, has a backbone, and grows hair at some point during its life. Female mammals have glands that can produce milk.

maritime hammock · *noun*
A predominantly evergreen hardwood forest growing on stabilized coastal dunes lying at varying distances from the shore.

montane · *adjective*
Of or inhabiting mountainous country.

native species · *noun*
Organisms that occur naturally in a given region through non-human introduction.

nocturnal · *adjective*
Active or occurring at night.

organism · *noun*
A living thing, such as an animal, plant, or micro-organism, capable of reproduction, growth, and maintenance.

omnivore · *noun*
An organism that regularly consumes plants, animals, algae, and fungi.

outcrop · *noun*
A place where bedrock naturally protrudes through the soil level.

peat · *noun*
Decaying plant matter typically found in wetlands like bogs and swamps.

photosynthesis · *noun*
The process by which plants make their own food using carbon dioxide, water, and sunlight.

pollinators · *noun*
An animal that causes plants to make fruit or seeds by moving pollen from one part of the flower of a plant to another part.

radiocarbon dating · *noun*
A method used for determining the age of organic materials by measuring the amount of carbon-14 left in the organism.

ungulate · *noun*
A hoofed mammal.

venomous · *adjective*
Of animals, especially snakes, capable of injecting venom by means of a bite or sting.

ANSWER KEY

PAGE 11 - HIDDEN OBJECTS

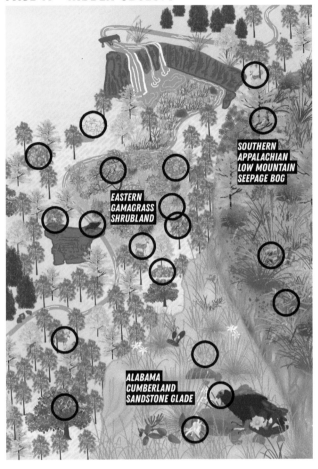

Labels on image:
- SOUTHERN APPALACHIAN LOW MOUNTAIN SEEPAGE BOG
- EASTERN GAMAGRASS SHRUBLAND
- ALABAMA CUMBERLAND SANDSTONE GLADE

PAGE 15 - PLANT IDENTIFICATION

Symmetry
Radial
D, E, G, H

Bilateral
B, F

Asymmetry
C

Color
White
E, H, B

Yellow
D, G

Violet
C, F

Pink
C, H

Leaf Shape
Linear
F

Oval
B, D

Egg
G

Spoon
E

Lance
C, H

Arrangement
Alternate (Alt.)
B, C, F

Opposite (Opp.)
D, G, H

Basal
E

PAGE 21 - WHAT SPECIES AM I?

D Alabama Heelsplitter

C Alabama Red-bellied Turtle

B Alabama Sturgeon

A (Fighting) Tarpon

F Gulf Saltmarsh Snake

E Largemouth Bass

PAGE 29 - WORD SEARCH

```
B W J Q W A T E R C R E S S D A R T E R
A O Y G J B F I G H T I N G T A R P O N
C G D B E L O I E K R U R O L E P O B W
H C R E L U R L P E D W Y P Q D L M H O
M C R A U A Y U D F U V F H I X H S E A
A R Q C Y B C B H O B L U E S H I N E R
N Q U H O B E K A W J A U R V C E L L C
S A T D R L A E B L N B L T V R E R S R
T P E L H G T G E B T G D G B S S P E E
P Z U E H J E Z M R A Z F R E S U B L S
A Y D R E A M Q L S U R J T Z A J G I S
R K C M G N C G N T E P W O L U G X T W
R I Z O N E U Q U O N L K I E R O L T A
O U P U S V O I N A R U E S G B T W E T
W Q T S L P L N T D I I H E L Z E E R T
E S T E R E D B E L L I E D T U R T L E
O I X V X F A C Q W N S T N P R I E M R
N O Z K K L A R G E M O U T H B A S S X
N O R T H E R N F L I C K E R T A N A U
N O M I R W P Z A W K R D U D I L S R W
```

EXPLORE FURTHER

BIOLOGICAL CLASSIFICATION *from page 2*

This book focuses on these three categories.

Groups organisms into categories.

What: Taxonomists classify plants and animals based on genetics and observable physical traits like having fur, gills, or feathers.

Why: Grouping species with similar makeup gives decision-makers the information they need for effective conservation planning.

Canines
Canidae

Gray Wolf
Canis lupus

Gray Wolf
Canis lupus

Red Fox
Vulpes vulpes

Red Wolf
Canis rufus

Red Wolf
Canis rufus

Red Wolf
Canis rufus

Family
Just like humans, plants and animals have families, too! Each family member is different but shares enough physical similarities to be grouped together.

Genus
A group of related living things made up of one or more species.

Species
A group of similar organisms that are able to reproduce.

Scientific names are based on a set of rules accepted worldwide:

Common Name	Family	Genus	Species
Yellowhammer	Woodpecker, *Picidae*	Colaptes	auratus
Yellowhammer	Sparrow, *Emberizidae*	Emberiza	citrinella

Common names are not reliable. In this example, using the common name "yellowhammer" could refer to either the woodpecker or the sparrow.

ECOLOGY LEVELS *from page 6*

Individual →	Population →	Community →	Habitat →	Ecosystem
A single member of a species.	Individuals of the same species in the same habitat.	Populations of several species in one habitat.	The physical site where an individual lives, like an address for a home. Habitat surrounds a population of one species.	A community of interacting organisms (living things like plants, animals, microbes) and their environment (nonliving things like sunlight, rainfall, temperature).

Examples:

Fowler's toad	All of the Fowler's toads in a given area	Fowler's toads + northern flickers + grasses in a given area	The toad's habitat could be a pond. Habitats range in size and can be as small as algae on a rock or an entire ocean.	Ecosystems can contain many habitats. The toad could live in an ecosystem including both a pond and forest habitat.

VIDEO RESOURCE
Key Ecology Terms for a breakdown of definitions • From Fuse School - Global Education
🌐 youtube.com/watch?v=E6WAQpRulhA

 WATCH

EXPLORE FURTHER

ECOSYSTEM INTERACTIONS *from page 10*

Ecosystems fall under two types and include both biotic and abiotic components:

TERRESTRIAL
Land-based environments like forests, grasslands, and deserts

AQUATIC
Water-based environments like lakes, ponds, rivers, oceans, and bogs

BIOTIC COMPONENTS
Parts of the Food Chain

 → →

PRODUCERS →   **CONSUMERS** →   **DECOMPOSERS**

The sun is the ulimate source of energy on Earth.

Organisms that produce their own food. Producers create food for themselves and provide energy for the rest of the ecosystem.

Organisms that depend on other organisms for food.

Bacteria and fungi that break down dead organisms into organic nutrients so that plants can make more food.

ABIOTIC COMPONENTS
- air
- soil
- water
- sunlight
- temperature
- minerals
- nutrients
- wind

Access to nonliving resources is limited!

Types of Consumers

Carnivores
an organism that eats meat

Predator
an animal that lives by killing and eating other animals

Some omnivores eat some carnivores.

Omnivores
an organism that eats meat and plants

Predator and prey

Herbivores
an organism that feeds mostly on plants

Prey
an animal that is hunted and killed by another for food

Competition
Within a given area, there may be limited resources like water, nutrients, and space, so living things have to compete for these resources. They do so by:

Direct competition - organisms interact with each other to obtain a resource
e.g., two different species who go after the same prey

Indirect competition - organisms affect each other's access to a resource in a secondhand way
e.g., a change in one species' population affects another.

Ecosystem Threats
- invasive species
- climate change
- natural disasters
- disease
- pollution
- human activity

Resource competition is further affected by external factors.

EXPLORE FURTHER

WEATHER VS. CLIMATE *from page 4*

WEATHER is the daily change in the atmosphere that includes conditions like temperature, precipitation, and wind. Weather lets us know what we should wear for the day!

Su Mo Tu We Tr Fr Sa

CLIMATE is the weather of a place over a period of time. Climate looks at weather patterns that could tell us about the effects on ecosystems, crop yields, human health, and other issues at regional and global levels.

30-year span

ECOREGIONS *from page 4*

What is an ecoregion?
Earth has a variety of landforms like deserts, oceans, and mountains, but plants and animals are not distributed evenly across these landscapes. There are some types of plants you wouldn't find in a desert because their food and water needs would not be met.

Instead, both living and nonliving things reside in areas based on climate, rock formations, type of soil, and water availability — this is what is known as an **ECOREGION** (short for ecological region).

Why are ecoregions important? Similar to taxonomy, studying areas with similar characteristics gives scientists the data they need to create best practices for sustainable use of the land.

GEOLOGY *from page 13*

Why geology is important
Not only does geology reveal the major events in Earth's history, but it is at the core of everyday life — it's in our cell phones, it helps us assess risks from natural disasters, and it is instrumental in the clean water and healthy food we consume.

How do scientists describe the age of rocks? Earth consists of layers of rock that have built up over time. Geologists look at fossils from these distinctive layers to establish a rock's age. A timeline describing these various ages is the:

GEOLOGIC TIME SCALE a chart containing the names and time ranges of the eons, eras, periods, and other divisions of geologic time.

Rocks, Minerals, and Elements

Sedimentary rocks are formed from pre-existing rocks or pieces of once-living organisms.	Rocks are made of one or more minerals.	Minerals are a collection of one or more elements stacked together in a crystal structure.	Elements are atoms. Different elements have different properties.
		Examples:	
Dolomite Limestone Shale	Sandstone Limestone Granite	Dolomite Quartz Calcite	Magnesium Calcium Silicon

Source: U.S. Geological Survey 🌐 usgs.gov

Paleozoic

Paleozoic and Precambrian

Mesozoic and Cenozoic

Geology of Alabama:

Cenozoic
0–65 million years ago

Mesozoic
65–248 million years ago

Paleozoic
248–590 million years ago

Precambrian
> 590 million years ago

View a detailed map of Alabama's geology
🌐 https://bit.ly/2ZSHP5v

EXPLORE FURTHER

ADDITIONAL WILD PLACES – NOTABLE MENTIONS

Cahaba River
One of the most biologically diverse rivers with more fish species per mile than any other river in the United States

Cane Creek Canyon Nature Preserve
700-acre private preserve featuring sandstone canyons

Sharp Bingham Mountain Preserve
Karst-type cave system

Sipsey Wilderness Area
Some of the last stands of virgin timber including rare species like the black warrior waterdog and the flattened musk turtle

Wheeler National Wildlife Refuge
Wintering home of the endangered whooping crane

CAHABA LILIES AT THE CAHABA RIVER

NOTES

CPSIA information can be obtained
at www.ICGtesting.com
Printed in the USA
BVHW020801191020
591318BV00002B/2